ANCIENT SUMER

THE HISTORY DETECTIVE INVESTIGATES

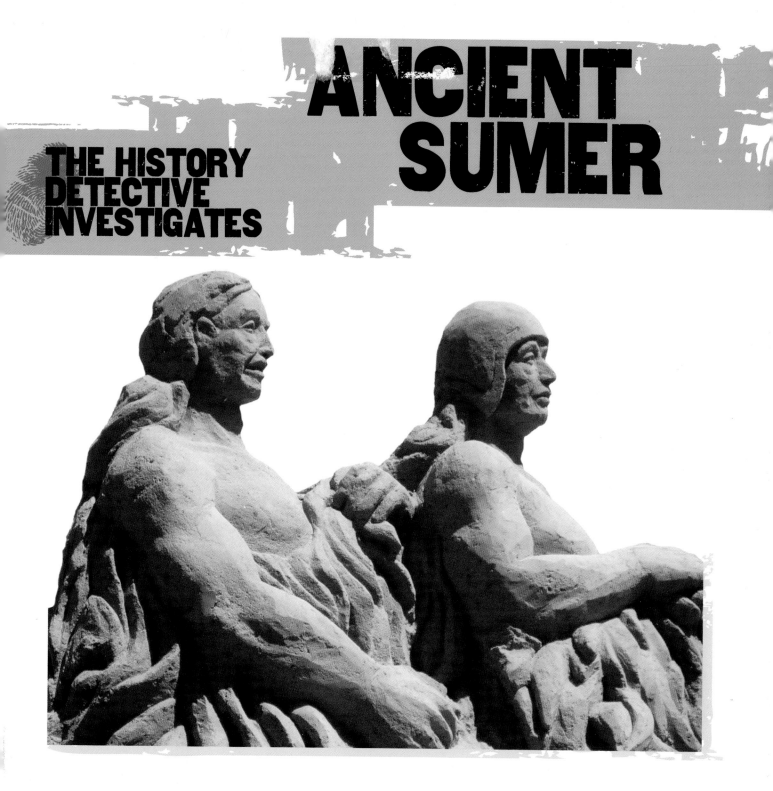

Kelly Davis

D0682125

First published in paperback in 2015 by Wayland
Copyright © Wayland 2015

Wayland, an imprint of Hachette Children's Group
Part of Hodder & Stoughton
Carmelite House, 50 Victoria Embankment
London EC4Y 0DZ

The History Detective Investigates series:
Ancient Egypt
Ancient Greece
Ancient Sumer
Anglo-Saxons
Benin 900-1897 CE
Castles
The Celts
The Civil Wars
Early Islamic Civilization
The Indus Valley
The Industrial Revolution
Local History
Mayan Civilization
Monarchs
The Normans and the Battle of Hastings
Post-War Britain
The Shang Dynasty of Ancient China
Stone Age to Iron Age
Tudor Exploration
Tudor Home
Tudor Medicine
Tudor Theatre
Tudor War
Victorian Crime
Victorian Factory
Victorian School
Victorian Transport
The Vikings
Weapons and Armour Through the Ages

Produced for Wayland by
White-Thomson Publishing Ltd
www.wtpub.co.uk
+44 (0)843 208 7460

Editor: Kelly Davis
Designer: Ian Winton
Cover design concept: Lisa Peacock
Consultant: Philip Parker
Proofreader: Lucy Ross

A catalogue record for this title is available from the British Library.

ISBN: 978-0-7502-9426-3
Library eBook ISBN: 978-0-7502-8526-1
Dewey Number: 935'.01-dc23

Printed in Malaysia

10 9 8 7 6 5 4 3 2 1

An Hachette UK company
www.hachette.co.uk
www.hachettechildrens.co.uk

Picture Acknowledgments: Chris Lee, 'Inspiring Creativity', www.chrislee.org/The New Art Gallery Walsall, Garman Ryan Collection: 7; **Stefan Chabluk:** 4, 17b; **The Bridgeman Art Library:** 21 (De Agostini Picture Library/M. Seemuller), 23 (De Agostini Picture Library/ M. Seemuller); **Corbis:** 12 (Corbis); **Dreamstime:** 25 (Sanjab), 28t (Kmiragaya); **Shutterstock:** 2 (Hadrian), 5t (Vladimir Korostyshevskiy), 20t (jsp); **Werner Forman Archive:** 8 (National Museum, Beirut, Lebanon), 9r (Otago Museum, Dunedin, New Zealand), 14 (British Museum, London), 17t (Charles University, Prague), 18 (British Museum, London), 26 (British Museum, London), 29 (Christie's, London); **Wikimedia:** cover t (Marie-Lan Nguyen), cover b (M. Lubinski), folios (Jmiall), 1 (Roger W. Haworth), 5b (Marie-Lan Nguyen), 6 (Dbachmann), 9l (Jmiall), 10 (M. Lubinski), 11 (Hardnfast), 13t (BabelStone), 13b (Michel wal), 15t (Gavin.collins), 15b (Daderot), 16t (Mbzt), 16b (Marie-Lan Nguyen), 19t (Marie-Lan Nguyen), 19b (Mike Peel), 20b (Daderot), 22 (Mbzt), 24 (Daderot), 27 (Mbzt), 28b (Wikimedia).

Right: These stones show examples of ancient Sumerian writing.

Previous page: This is a modern sculpture of ancient Sumerians.

Cover (top): Detail from the Standard of Ur.

Cover (bottom): These are the ruins of the royal palace of Ur.

CONTENTS

Words in **bold** can be found in the glossary on page 30.

The history detective Sherlock Bones will help you to find clues and collect evidence about ancient Sumer. Wherever you see one of Sherlock's paw-prints, you will find a mystery to solve. The answers are on page 31.

WHO WERE THE ANCIENT SUMERIANS?

The ancient Sumerians were extremely clever, inventive people who had a huge effect on the world we live in today. They lived in ancient Sumer, an area that is now part of southern Iraq, bounded by the River Euphrates and the River Tigris. The Greeks later named this region Mesopotamia, meaning 'the land between the rivers'.

DETECTIVE WORK

Find out about the history of ancient Sumer by looking at a British Museum timeline: www.mesopotamia.co.uk/time/explore/frame_sum.html

This map shows ancient Sumer, with its main cities, and the neighbouring areas of Akkad and Elam.

Between 6000 and 5000 BCE, a new **culture** appeared in southern Mesopotamia. This culture is called the Ubaid period, after the village of al-Ubaid, where **archaeologists** first discovered Ubaidian painted pottery. Although there was little rain, the Ubaidians knew how to **irrigate** the land, using water from the rivers, and they built settlements at Eridu. This early culture lasted until about 4000 BCE.

From 4000 BCE onwards, the Sumerian civilization became established. Sumerians built large cities and temples, and invented a written script to record their language. People also had particular jobs – for example, as farmers, potters, priests and merchants. The city of Uruk was home to more than 50,000 people (the biggest city in the world at that time) and gave its name to the Uruk period, which lasted from 4000 to 3000 BCE. During this period, the cities grew and became **city-states**.

Why did the Greeks call this region Mesopotamia?

The Uruk period was followed by the Early Dynastic period (2900–2300 BCE). Then, in around 2300 BCE, the Sumerians were conquered by the Akkadians, who came from the city of Akkad to the north. The Akkadians ruled for around 200 years, though Sumerian was still used alongside the Akkadian language.

From about 2100 BCE, there was a short Sumerian revival, under Gudea (ruler of the city-state of Lagash). After Gudea died in battle, Lagash lost its power and was replaced as the most important city-state by Ur, whose ruler Ur-Nammu controlled most of ancient Sumer. Ur-Nammu reigned for around seventeen years, and ordered the building of several temples. He was followed by his son, Shulgi.

This carved head of an Akkadian ruler was made in 2300 BCE.

Archaeologists have found several versions of the Sumerian King List. The list becomes roughly historically accurate from the Third **Dynasty** of Uruk (2355–2330 BCE) onwards.

This statue of Gudea is dated around 2100 BCE.

More than 4,000 years ago, King Shulgi wrote:

'Now, I swear by the sun god Utu on this very day … that I, the firstborn son, am a fashioner of words, a composer of songs, a composer of words, and that they will recite my songs as heavenly writings, and that they will bow down before my words…'

WHAT DID THE ANCIENT SUMERIANS INVENT?

Sumerian inventions changed the course of human history. They included the wheel, the first writing system, many mathematical ideas, and several farming and metalworking techniques.

The wheel was probably invented in around 4000 BCE in ancient Sumer, in order to make pottery. Many experts believe the potter's wheel was later enlarged, placed on its side, and used to make carts and wagons. The earliest wheels were made of wood, which rots away, so the only evidence we have is painted or carved images and pottery models of wheeled vehicles.

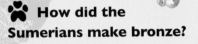 **How did the Sumerians make bronze?**

Early Sumerians used small clay tokens to represent **goods**, and these tokens were kept in large, sealed clay containers. The Sumerians showed the number of tokens by pressing small pictures of them on the outside with a hollow reed stem. Eventually they stopped using clay tokens, and simply impressed the symbols on to wet clay. By around 3000 BCE, they started using a wedge-shaped reed stem that could be pushed into the clay to produce wedge-shaped **cuneiform** symbols (from the Latin word *cuneus*, meaning 'wedge'). This was the first writing system (see pages 16-17).

This detail from the Standard of Ur (dated around 2500 BCE) shows a king in a wheeled chariot.

The Sumerians used symbols to represent numbers of clay tokens and created a system of mathematics based on multiples of 6 and 10. As early as 2600 BCE, they were writing multiplication tables on clay tablets. They also invented units of measurement for area, length and volume.

By recording their observations of the night sky, the Sumerians invented the science of **astronomy**. They mapped the stars and noted the movements of the Sun, the Moon and the five visible planets (Venus, Jupiter, Saturn, Mercury and Mars).

The inhabitants of ancient Sumer were also the first people to use several farming techniques, including irrigation. They were irrigating their crops from around 5000 BCE onwards. This enabled them to grow crops on a large scale, to feed the growing populations in their settlements (see pages 14-15). Finally, the Sumerians may have been the first people to add tin to copper in order to make bronze, which was much harder than copper. They used bronze to make tools and weapons.

This is a bronze socket axe head, another Sumerian invention. The socket slipped over the wooden axe handle, and was held on with short metal pins or bolts.

DETECTIVE WORK

Find out more about Sumerian mathematics by visiting www.storyofmathematics. com/sumerian.html

Samuel Noah Kramer was an expert on the ancient Sumerians. In 1963, he wrote:

'The people of Sumer had an unusual flair for technological invention… They devised such useful tools, skills, and techniques as the potter's wheel, the wagon wheel, the plow, the sailboat, the arch, the vault, the dome, casting in copper and bronze, riveting, brazing and soldering, sculpture in stone, engraving, and inlay.'

WHAT WAS DAILY LIFE LIKE IN ANCIENT SUMER?

By around 3000 BCE, the Sumerians were living in large city-states, such as Kish and Ur. Each one had a walled city with a temple in the centre, dedicated to that city's god. Land, farms, people and animals all belonged to the god, and food was rationed out to members of the community by the priests who ran the temple.

The city-state was ruled by a king, called a *lugal*. The upper class was made up of priests, nobles and wealthy landowners, and the commoners were farmers, traders and craftspeople. There were also slaves, captured from other city-states and the surrounding area.

Ordinary city-dwelling Sumerians lived in one-roomed mud-brick houses, while wealthier families had bigger, multi-storeyed homes with several rooms, usually surrounding a courtyard or garden. They cooked over an open fire, and slept on bundles of reeds.

Here are some Sumerian **proverbs**. Most of them still make a lot of sense!

Wealth is hard to come by, but poverty is always at hand.
He who acquires many things must keep close watch over them.
He who drinks too much beer must drink water.
He who eats too much will not be able to sleep.

DETECTIVE WORK

Visit this website to find out what wealthy Sumerians ate at a feast: http://mesopotamia. lib.uchicago.edu/ mesopotamialife/article. php?theme=DailyLife

This pottery jug was found in Lagash. It was used during the Early Dynastic period (2900–2300 BCE).

Early Sumerians wore sheepskin skirts and cloaks with the wool combed into tufts on the outside. After about 2500 BCE, they started to weave woollen fabric and kept the tufted effect by sewing on tufts or weaving loops into the fabric. Wealthy men and women wore jewellery, clothes made from colourful woven linen or wool, and leather shoes. Poorer people wore simple tunics and reed sandals. After about 2370 BCE, people started to wear draped linen garments, often edged with tassels or a fringe.

Marriages were arranged by the families of the bride and groom, and most women stayed at home to cook, clean and look after their children. Education was expensive so only boys from wealthy families were sent to school and learned to read and write. Some of them became **scribes**.

This sculpture, dating back to 2500 BCE, shows a Sumerian man's clothes and hairstyle.

Most Sumerians didn't travel much. However, traders transported goods on the canals that surrounded many of the city-states and on the roads, using wheeled carts drawn by donkeys. They also sailed down the rivers to trade their cloth and grain for copper, silver, soapstone, shells and other valuable items, travelling as far as India and the eastern Mediterranean.

Which deep blue, semi-precious stone was used in Sumerian jewellery?

This head-dress and necklace, made of gold, lapis lazuli (blue) and carnelian (red), was found in a royal tomb. It was worn by one of the queen's female attendants in around 2500 BCE.

HOW DID ANCIENT SUMERIANS BUILD?

As there was very little stone in ancient Sumer, the early Sumerians made their houses and temples out of sun-baked mud-brick. These buildings did not last long, and the Sumerians periodically destroyed them and built new houses and temples on top. The repeated levelling and building eventually formed hills, called tells.

As time went on, Sumerians began to use wooden moulds to make bricks that looked like loaves of bread. Later still, they started using **kilns** to fire the bricks. This enabled them to make longer-lasting buildings. They also used a sticky, black petroleum-based substance called bitumen to fill the gaps between the bricks and give them a water-resistant coating.

Ordinary people in the cities lived in mud-brick houses crammed together in narrow, twisted streets. Outside the city walls, farmers and fishermen lived in small reed huts, plastered with clay.

From 4000 BCE onwards, the early Sumerians were building large temples on mud-brick platforms. The oldest one found so far was built at Eridu. By around 2100 BCE, these temples had become huge structures known as **ziggurats**, which towered above the cities. A ziggurat had three platforms, each one smaller than the one below, with a temple to a god or goddess at the top. The top could be reached by a steep staircase at the front, which some historians think only priests were allowed to use.

How did the Sumerians protect their buildings from the effects of water?

The ruins of the royal palace of Ur are in the foreground, showing the remaining brickwork, with the ziggurat in the background.

The most famous ziggurat is the one in the city of Ur. The building work started in around 2100 BCE, under King Ur-Nammu, and was finished by his son King Shulgi. The central part was made of mud-bricks, covered with a layer of baked bricks, which had been fired to protect them against damp. Small holes were made to allow moisture to **evaporate** from the inner core.

DETECTIVE WORK

Find out how hard it was to organize the building of a ziggurat by visiting www.mesopotamia.co.uk/ ziggurats/challenge/ cha_set.html

This is the reconstructed ziggurat at Ur, with part of the old temple visible at the top.

Buttress

Old temple

Staircase

On either side of the steep staircase at the front there were **buttresses**. A blue-**glazed** brick has been found at Ur and this may have come from the temple at the top. The ruins indicate that the Sumerians knew how to build arches and domes. They also decorated their buildings with **mosaic**, made by inserting clay cones with coloured bases into the walls.

The famous crime writer Agatha Christie met an archaeologist called Max Mallowan (who became her husband in 1930) at the Ur **excavations**. She later wrote a novel entitled *Murder in Mesopotamia* and commented:

'I fell in love with Ur, with its beautiful evenings, the ziggurat standing up, faintly shadowed…The lure of the past came up to grab me. To see a dagger slowly appearing, with its gold glint, through the sand was romantic.'

WHO FOUND THE ROYAL TOMBS OF UR?

The ruins of the city of Ur (including the ziggurat) were first discovered by J.G. Taylor in 1854. However, Taylor wasn't a trained archaeologist and many of the remains were damaged. Nearly 70 years later, in 1922, an English archaeologist called Leonard Woolley organized further excavations.

In 1923, Woolley and his team decided to dig two large **trenches** near the ruined ziggurat. In the first week they made some exciting discoveries, including gold jewellery and evidence of burials and ancient buildings.

The excavations continued for several years, and in 1927 Woolley's team found another 300 graves. Four of them were very different from the others. They were **tombs** with several rooms, rather than simple pits. Each one contained many bodies, surrounded by extraordinary objects. Woolley called them the 'royal tombs' and newspapers all over the world reported the amazing finds.

This beautiful gold, copper and lapis lazuli sculpture, discovered in one of the royal tombs, depicts a ram caught in a bush.

In January 1928, having entered the tomb of Queen Pu-abi, Woolley sent a telegram in Latin. The translation reads:

'I found the intact tomb, stone built and vaulted over with bricks of Queen Shubad (Pu-abi) adorned with a dress in which gems, flower crowns and animal figures are woven. Tomb magnificent with jewels and golden cups.'

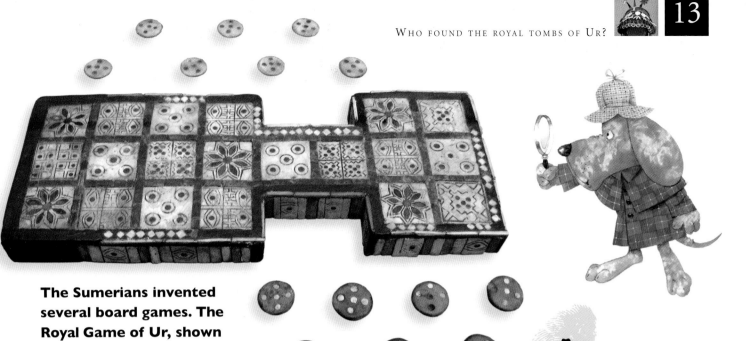

The Sumerians invented several board games. The Royal Game of Ur, shown here, was found in one of the royal tombs.

How many people played the Royal Game of Ur?

Woolley finished his excavations at Ur in 1934, having found a total of 1,850 burials. Seventeen of them were royal tombs, dating back to around 2600 BCE. Woolley gave each one a PG (private grave) number. PG1237 was the biggest, and it contained the bodies of 68 women and six men. The women all wore head-dresses made of gold, silver and lapis lazuli, and the men had weapons and seemed to be guarding the tomb's entrance. Woolley believed the neat arrangement of the bodies, and the cups next to them, showed that they must have willingly drunk poison and waited for death.

DETECTIVE WORK

Explore the royal tombs of Ur for yourself by visiting www. mesopotamia.co.uk/ tombs/explore/exp_ set.html

One of the most important finds was the **Standard of Ur**, a box decorated with mosaic pictures that tell us a lot about life in ancient Sumer. One side shows the Sumerians fighting battles; the other, known as the 'Peace side', shows them farming, feasting and playing music.

This is a detail from the 'Peace side' of the Standard of Ur.

HOW DID ANCIENT SUMERIANS FARM?

Ancient Sumer was located between the River Tigris and the River Euphrates and the soil was therefore very damp and fertile. However, much of the land was marshy and there was frequent flooding. In order to farm successfully, the people had to build huge banks along the rivers to control the floodwaters. They also had to drain the marshes, and dig irrigation canals and ditches. Laws were passed requiring farmers to help dig new canals and repair old ones when necessary.

The most important crops were wheat and barley, and Sumerians invented a seeder plough that was much more efficient than planting by hand. The ox pulled the plough, and seed dropped down a central funnel positioned on the plough, into the **furrow**. The Sumerians invented many other farming tools, including the rake, sickle and shovel. Some tools were made of wood, but by 3000 BCE bronze was used to make stronger implements.

DETECTIVE WORK

Find out more about Sumerian farming by playing this irrigation game: www.mesopotamia.co.uk/geography/challenge/cha_set.html

What did the ancient Sumerians use barley for?

This stone carving from Uruk (dated around 3000 BCE) shows a man walking beside an ox. Another person sits astride the animal's neck.

Wheat and barley were harvested and made into bread, beer and a kind of porridge. Any grain that was not needed for food could be traded for other goods. The Sumerians also grew chickpeas, lentils, onions, garlic, leeks, apples, plums, grapes, dates and many other crops. Growing food on a large scale enabled them to feed the expanding populations in their city-states. Every year, the amount of produce was recorded by harvest supervisors. It was then rationed out each month to members of the community.

Ancient Sumerians kept farm animals as well as growing crops. They had sheep, goats and cattle to provide milk, meat and skins. Oxen were used to pull ploughs and donkeys to transport goods.

Here are some lines from an ancient Sumerian hymn to Ninkasi, goddess of brewing, which describes the way the Sumerians made beer. The 'cooked mash' was twice-baked barley bread, mixed with honey and dates:

Ninkasi, you are the one who spreads the cooked mash on large reed mats,
Coolness overcomes...
   You are the one who holds with both hands the great sweetwort,
Brewing [it] with honey [and] wine...
The fermenting vat, which makes a pleasant sound,
You place appropriately on [top of] a large collector vat.

▲ **This is an account of monthly barley rations issued to adults and children, written on a clay tablet in around 2350 BCE.**

This bronze calf was made in about 2400 BCE.

HOW DID ANCIENT SUMERIANS WRITE?

We know so much about the Sumerians because they developed the art of writing, and could therefore leave permanent records. This is why we know how they lived, and what they thought and felt. Writing was perhaps their most important achievement.

Before about 3300 BCE, the Sumerians pressed small pictures into soft clay to keep records of goods bought and sold. Gradually they started using other picture **symbols** that looked like what they represented – for example, two wavy lines meant 'water' or 'stream'.

This is a tablet from the Uruk period (4000–3000 BCE), showing the pictures used before the development of cuneiform.

Which pictures can you identify on this tablet?

DETECTIVE WORK

Find out more about the history of writing from: www.britishmuseum.org/explore/themes/writing/historic_writing.aspx Write your own name in cuneiform by visiting: www.penn.museum/cgi/cuneiform.cgi

This Sumerian contract of sale for a field and a house is written in pre-cuneiform script.

In about 3000 BCE, the Sumerians started using the wedge-shaped end of a hollow reed stem, called a **stylus**, to impress the symbols into clay. They also began to arrange them in rows, moving from left to right (rather than top to bottom). At the same time, the strokes making up the signs became wedge-shaped. This type of writing, known as cuneiform, wasn't only used to keep records of accounts. By 2800 BCE, Sumerians were writing prayers, poems, stories, songs, recipes and letters. The clay cuneiform tablets were then fired in kilns to preserve them, creating a lasting record.

This contract, recording the sale of a slave, was written in cuneiform in around 2300 BCE:

'Sini-Ishtar has bought a slave, Ea-tappi by name, from Ilu-elatti, and Akhia, his son, and has paid ten shekels of Silver, the price agreed… In the presence of … Likulubishtum, son of Appa, the scribe, who sealed it with the seal of the witnesses.'

Scribes started putting symbols together to make other words. For instance, the sign for 'head' had some lines added to become 'mouth'. Then the symbols for 'mouth' and 'bread' were combined to make 'eat'.

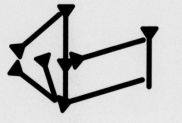

◀ **This 'envelope and letter' dates from around 3000 BCE. The 'envelope' shows the marks of the seal used by the sender.**

▼ **This illustration shows how the ancient Sumerians put symbols together to form new words.**

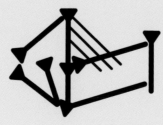

Head   **Mouth**   **To eat**

WHO WAS GILGAMESH?

Gilgamesh is often described as 'the first superhero' and a 'hero-king'. He is mentioned in the Sumerian King List (written around 2100 BCE) but he doesn't sound like a real person, as he supposedly ruled Uruk for 126 years! One version of the story says his mother was the goddess Ninsun and his father was a spirit, who became a priest; and later Sumerian sources describe Gilgamesh as a 'king of the underworld' (hell).

In fact, Gilgamesh may really have been the fifth king of Uruk, who ruled around 2700 BCE. **Inscriptions** have been found saying that Gilgamesh built the great walls of Uruk, and in 2003 some German archaeologists announced that they had found his tomb.

Which Gilgamesh tablet told the story of a great flood?

DETECTIVE WORK

Click on this link to read about the German expedition that claimed to have found Gilgamesh's tomb (and the city of Uruk) under the River Euphrates:
http://news.bbc.co.uk/1/hi/sci/tech/2982891.stm

This imprint from a carved seal, dated around 800 BCE, shows Gilgamesh as a bearded hero, kneeling and holding a lion above his head.

The *Epic of Gilgamesh* is one of the earliest recorded stories, and there are versions dating back to around 2100 BCE. It tells five stories about the hero-king of Uruk, including his battles with demons, his journey to a cedar forest, and his adventures in heaven and the underworld. The fullest version of the *Epic of Gilgamesh* was written in around 1800 BCE on twelve clay tablets. These were found in the library of the Assyrian king Ashurbanipal, who reigned from 668 to 627 BCE.

The eleventh tablet describes how Gilgamesh met Utnapishtim, who was warned by the gods that they were planning to send a great flood. Utnapishtim made a boat to hold his family, his possessions, and many animals. All other human beings were killed in the six-day flood, but Utnapishtim's boat landed on the mountain of Nimush. This story sounds very like many other flood myths from ancient cultures, especially the Bible story of Noah. In 1872, an assistant at the British Museum called George Smith read the text for the first time and apparently got so excited that he 'jumped up and rushed about the room' and 'began to undress himself'!

This is the top of a mace dedicated to Gilgamesh by Urdun, an official in Lagash.

The *Epic of Gilgamesh* begins:

'I will proclaim to the world the deeds of Gilgamesh. This was the man to whom all things were known; this was the king who knew the countries of the world. He was wise, he saw mysteries and knew secret things, he brought us a tale of the days before the flood.'

This is the eleventh Gilgamesh tablet, known as 'The Flood Tablet'. The Sumerian King List mentions a Great Flood, and says that eight kings reigned before it. Gilgamesh is listed as one of the post-Flood rulers.

WHAT ART DID ANCIENT SUMERIANS CREATE?

The Sumerians created many beautiful artworks, including sculptures, pottery, jewellery, mosaics and musical instruments. Their art often showed religious subjects such as gods, goddesses and spirits.

They also made votive figures. These were small statues that they left in temples, probably to stand in for real worshippers. Some early statues (dated 3500–3000 BCE) are very realistic, while later votive figures are less realistic and have unusually big eyes.

There was very little stone in ancient Sumer so they made most of their art objects from clay, wood and metals (including gold, silver and copper). They also carved alabaster, limestone, gypsum and marble, often using shell, lapis lazuli and gold to add inlaid details and decoration.

By about 3000 BCE, the Sumerians had learnt how to make metal statues and other artworks, using the 'lost wax process'. This meant making an object out of wax, covering it with concrete, then heating the concrete so that the wax melted and ran out. The cavity was filled with molten metal, which solidified. The lioness below was produced in this way.

This votive statue dates back to around 2400 BCE.

This copper alloy lioness was made in about 2100 BCE.

Cylinder seals were a very common form of art, and they were invented in ancient Sumer in around 3400 BCE (see picture on page 29). The Sumerians made these seals from baked clay or carved them from stone. They usually had a hole through the centre so that the owner could wear the seal on a string or pin. When rolled on wet clay, the cylinder left a raised picture. This represented the person's signature. However, seals were also used as a form of jewellery.

Musical instruments were another form of Sumerian art. The Sumerians enjoyed playing music at religious festivals and ceremonies, and they made instruments such as drums, tambourines, pipes, harps and lyres. Many of these were richly decorated.

This bull's head decorated a harp that was found in one of the royal tombs at Ur. It was made between 2800 and 2300 BCE.

DETECTIVE WORK

Read about the restoration of a lyre found by Leonard Woolley by visiting www.penn.museum/sites/iraq/?page_id=58

What do you think the bull's head is decorated with?

In his memoirs, Max Mallowan, an archaeologist at the Ur excavations, recalled that one of the royal tombs:

'...appeared, when exposed, to be a golden carpet ornamented with the beech leaf head-dresses of the ladies of the court, and overlaid by gold and silver harps and lyres which had played the funeral **dirge** to the end.'

HOW DID ANCIENT SUMERIANS FIGHT?

It is often claimed that the ancient Sumerians spent a lot of time fighting each other. However, the Uruk period, which lasted from around 4000 to 3000 BCE, was largely peaceful. It was only later that war became a feature of life in ancient Sumer.

The first known record of a Sumerian war is the **Stele** of Vultures (dated around 2450 BCE). This stone carving records the victory of King Eannatum of Lagash over the neighbouring city-state of Umma. The first three pieces of the original stone slab were found in 1881 in Girsu (now Tello, Iraq), by a French archaeologist called Ernest de Sarzec.

In his book *The Ancient World* (2007), Richard A. Gabriel wrote:

'It was in ancient Sumer that the first detailed records of military campaigns written on clay or carved in stone appeared. No society of the Early and Middle Bronze ages was more advanced in the design and application of military technology and technique than Sumer.'

This is a piece of the Stele of Vultures, so-called because it shows vultures carrying off the heads of the defeated soldiers.

There were almost constant wars from around 3000 BCE onwards (often over control of land and water supplies) and the Sumerians became experts in the art of warfare. Each city-state had a trained army and they frequently fought each other. **Sieges** sometimes went on for very long periods, cutting off the besieged city until the people inside began to starve. Meanwhile, the besieging army built ladders (and possibly towers) in order to get over the high city walls.

🐾 **Why do you think there were so many wars after 3000 BCE?**

Ordinary soldiers had leather helmets and capes, sometimes covered with bronze discs, which gave some protection against blades. They also carried rectangular shields, and some of the higher-ranking soldiers had copper helmets. The Sumerians had many types of weapon including clubs, spears, swords, axes and daggers. They may also have used slings to fire stones at the enemy.

Sumerian metalworkers were skilled at making weapons, like this dagger, found in one of the royal tombs at Ur.

From the Stele of Vultures and the Standard of Ur (see pages 12-13), we know the Sumerians used military tactics, such as arranging spearmen in a block called a phalanx. Having invented the wheel, they were able to build carts and chariots that could carry military equipment. Chariots were also used in battle, with one man driving and another one standing behind him, throwing spears at the enemy troops.

DETECTIVE WORK

Click on this link to see a bronze Sumerian spearhead, dated between 2600 and 2500 BCE. http://mesopotamia. lib.uchicago.edu/ learningcollection/search. php?a_object_type_ browse=Tools&lcid=127

WHAT DID ANCIENT SUMERIANS BELIEVE IN?

The Sumerians believed in deities, who represented different aspects of nature, such as the Sun and Moon, storms and floods. These deities were worshipped at the temples and also at small shrines in people's homes. Priests looked after the gods – washing and clothing the statues and even leaving food for them. There were also regular festivals and ceremonies in their honour, when the gods' statues were carried in processions.

Each city-state was protected by a particular deity, and the people of that city mainly prayed to that god to protect their city and give them a good harvest. For instance, Inanna (goddess of love, **fertility** and war) was worshipped by the people of Uruk. The ruler of the city acted as a link between the god and the people. It was his duty to organize the building and repair of temples.

This sculpture of a god holding a nail was made in about 2100 BCE. It was probably used in a ceremony when a temple was built or repaired. It has an inscription linking it to Gudea, ruler of the city-state of Lagash. The inscribed nail is supported by a god, who is shown wearing a characteristic horned head-dress.

Here is part of a translation of an ancient Sumerian hymn to Inanna:

'The great queen of heaven,
Inanna,
I will hail!
The pure torch lit in the sky,
The heavenly light, lighting
    like day,
The great queen of heaven,
    Inanna,
I will hail!
The holy one,
Queen awe-laden
Of the Anunnaki,
Noblest one in heaven and
    earth,
Crowned with great horns,
Oldest child of the Moon,
Inanna,
I will hail!'

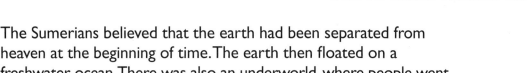

The Sumerians believed that the earth had been separated from heaven at the beginning of time. The earth then floated on a freshwater ocean. There was also an underworld, where people went after they died. The Sumerians therefore buried people with clothes, jewellery, food and anything else that they might need in the afterlife.

This sculpture shows an ancient Sumerian Anunnaki with the head of a bird.

DETECTIVE WORK

Find out more about Sumerian gods, goddesses and demons by visiting www.mesopotamia.co.uk/gods/explore/exp_set.html

Were all the gods and goddesses equally important?

The most important Sumerian deities were An (sky god and ruler of all the other gods), Enlil (god of the air), Enki (god of water, wisdom, farming and building), and Utu (god of the sun, truth and justice). In Sumerian stories, the gods often acted in a very human way – fighting, falling in love, and feeling jealous, sad or happy. According to some sources, the Anunnaki were gods of fertility, who later became judges in the underworld.

WHY DID ANCIENT SUMER END?

Between 2100 and 2000 BCE, the kings of Ur gradually gained control of more and more territory until they ruled the whole of ancient Sumer as well as much of Akkad. However, the Sumerian civilization suddenly ended in 2004 BCE, when the Elamites came from the east and destroyed the city of Ur.

How did the Elamites overcome such a powerful civilization? Many experts believe that the Sumerians were weakened by the constant fighting between their city-states, which had continued for the previous 500 years. There were also local uprisings and some of the Sumerian cities started refusing to pay taxes. In addition, there were raids by the Amorites (who cut off the food supply to Ur).

This stone carving, found at Nineveh in Assyria, shows the Elamites getting ready for war.

Here are some lines from a 'Lament for Ur', a poem written about the destruction of the city.

*'For the gods have
    abandoned us,
like migrating birds they
    have gone.
Ur is destroyed, bitter is
    its lament
The country's blood now fills
    its holes like hot bronze in
    a mould.
Bodies dissolve like fat in
    the sun. Our temple is
    destroyed.
Smoke lies on our city like
    a shroud.
Blood flows as the river does,
the lamenting of men and
    women,
sadness abounds,
Ur is no more.'*

Other researchers believe that the population gradually shrank because of a **drought** lasting between 200 and 300 years. Still others think the Sumerians' use of irrigation made the soil too salty. When fields are continually irrigated, the water evaporates, leaving behind a layer of salt; and there are references in ancient Sumerian writings to the earth turning white. The only way of solving the problem is to leave the land un-irrigated for several years and allow the rain to wash the salt down through the soil. Instead of doing this, the Sumerians gradually started growing more barley and less wheat because barley is more tolerant of salt. Nevertheless, even the barley crop eventually shrank, and many Sumerians apparently started to suffer from disease and hunger. This may be another reason why they were finally overcome by the Elamites.

The Elamites only ruled briefly. They were driven out in turn by the Amorites. Under the Amorites, land and people were no longer owned by temples. Farmers could now work for themselves and sell their own produce. But people still believed in the Sumerian gods, and used the Sumerian language for religious and legal purposes.

By around 1900 BCE, the Amorites had created the First Dynasty of Babylon, based in Babylon (to the west of Kish). The most powerful Babylonian king was Hammurabi, who reigned from 1792 to 1750 BCE. He issued a set of written laws, known as the Code of Hammurabi, for all his people.

This carving shows Hammurabi (standing), receiving his symbols of royal power from Shamash (the Babylonian sun god). Hammurabi holds his hands over his mouth as a sign of prayer.

When was the city of Ur destroyed?

DETECTIVE WORK

Learn more about the Amorites by visiting: www.historyfiles.co.uk/ KingListsMiddEast/ MesopotamiaAmorites.htm

YOUR PROJECT

By now you will have realized that the Sumerians were extraordinary people, who established a very advanced civilization. For your project, you might want to research one of their achievements, such as Sumerian art, astronomy, writing or mathematics.

If you live in or near London, you could look at the ancient Sumerian collection in the British Museum to gather information on your chosen subject. You might want to make notes and sketch some of the objects. If you live too far away, you can make a virtual visit by going to www.mesopotamia.co.uk/menu.html

This fired clay tablet is an example of ancient Sumerian cuneiform.

Alternatively, you could find out more about the archaeologists who have pieced together the story of the Sumerians. Leonard Woolley is the most famous, but it was actually a Frenchman called Ernest de Sarzec who found the first evidence of ancient Sumer. Or you may enjoy comparing the Sumerians with another culture, such as the ancient Egyptians. Find out how the two cultures differed, and how they resembled each other.

You might have your own ideas for a project, but whatever you decide, remember it is your project, so choose something that interests you. Good luck!

This photograph shows Leonard Woolley (left) and T.E. Lawrence at an excavation in Syria, between 1912 and 1914.

Project presentation

- Do plenty of research before you begin. Use the Internet and your local or school library.

- Experiment with different styles of writing. You don't have to stick to a descriptive style. You could also write diary entries as if you were a Sumerian scribe, priest or farmer. Or you could imagine yourself as an archaeologist excavating an ancient Sumerian site and writing letters and reports on your discoveries. If there are a lot of dates to be included, you could present some of the information as a timeline.

- Try making your own miniature ziggurat, using modelling clay. Imagine having to make all those mud-bricks!

- Collect as many pictures as you can to illustrate your project. Print off images from the Internet. Buy postcards from museums.

Find examples of Sumerian cylinder seals in books or on the Internet. This one is dated 2300–2100 BCE and shows a god's attendant.

GLOSSARY

alloy A metal made by melting and mixing two or more metals, or a metal and a non-metal, together.

archaeologist A person who studies past human life by digging up ancient bones, tools and other remains.

astronomy The study of the sun, moon, stars and planets.

BCE Before Common Era; before the birth of Christ.

buttress A stone or brick support for a wall.

city-state A city with surrounding territory that has its own government.

culture The ideas, customs and behaviour of a group of people.

cuneiform An ancient writing system using wedge-shaped characters.

deity A god or goddess.

dirge A slow, sad song played at a funeral.

drought A long period without rainfall.

dynasty A series of rulers from the same family.

evaporate To turn from liquid into moisture; to lose moisture.

excavation The process of digging up ancient remains.

fertility (Of a person) The ability to give birth; (of land) the ability to grow crops.

furrow A long narrow hollow made by a plough, in which to plant seeds.

glaze A decorative, coloured coating on pottery.

goods Items that are produced, transported and traded.

inscription Words that have been written on or cut into a hard surface.

irrigate Supply water to help crops grow, using pipes or channels.

kiln A type of oven used to fire (bake) pottery at high temperatures.

mace A heavy club, sometimes with a spiked metal head.

marsh An area of low-lying land that is frequently flooded or waterlogged.

mosaic A picture or pattern made by arranging small, coloured pieces next to each other.

proverb A short wise saying.

scribe A person who wrote and copied documents.

shrine A place where a god is worshipped.

siege Surrounding a city, town or fortress with an army that wishes to capture it.

Standard of Ur A box found at Ur, decorated with mosaic pictures showing life in ancient Sumer.

stele A large stone slab with writing (and sometimes pictures) carved on its surface.

stylus A sharp pointed writing instrument such as a cut reed stem.

symbol A mark or character used to represent something.

tomb A burial place with one or more rooms.

trench A long narrow ditch or hollow in the ground.

ziggurat A stepped temple with a series of platforms, each smaller than the one below.

ANSWERS

Page 4: The Greeks called this region Mesopotamia (meaning 'the land between two rivers') because it was between the Tigris and the Euphrates.

Page 6: The Sumerians added tin to copper to make bronze.

Page 9: The deep blue, semi-precious stone used in Sumerian jewellery was lapis lazuli.

Page 10: The Sumerians protected their buildings from the effects of water by using fired bricks and bitumen, and by making holes to let moisture evaporate.

Page 13: Two people played the Royal Game of Ur by moving their counters around the board.

Page 14: The Sumerians used barley to make bread, porridge and beer.

Page 16: The pictures may represent: a hand; a sickle (a tool used to cut wheat); a tree or plant; a bunch of grapes or perhaps some wheat; and a rake.

Page 18: The eleventh Gilgamesh tablet tells the story of a great flood.

Page 21: The bull's head is decorated with gold, lapis lazuli and possibly shell.

Page 22: The city-states grew larger and this led to disputes as they tried to take over each other's territory and fought over access to water.

Page 25: No, the Sumerian gods were not all equal. An (the sky god) ruled over the others.

Page 27: The city of Ur was destroyed in 2004 BCE by the Elamites.

FURTHER INFORMATION

Books to read

Mesopotamia (Eyewitness) by Philip Steele (Dorling Kindersley, 2007)

Mesopotamia (Excavating the Past) by Jane Shuter (Heinemann, 2006)

Mesopotamia: What Life Was Like in Ancient Sumer, Babylon and Assyria (Find Out About) by Lorna Oakes (Southwater, 2004)

Websites

www.britannica.com/EBchecked/topic/573176/Sumer

www.penn.museum

www.britishmuseum.org

Note to parents and teachers: Every effort has been made by the publishers to ensure that these websites are suitable for children. However, because of the nature of the Internet, it is impossible to guarantee that the contents of these sites will not be altered. We strongly advise that Internet access is supervised by a responsible adult.

Place to visit
British Museum, London WC1B 3DG

INDEX

Numbers in **bold** refer to pictures and captions